SCHIRMER'S LIBRARY OF MUSICAL CLASSICS

Vol. 170

HENRI HERZ

Scales and Exercises

For the Piano

NEW AND AUGMENTED EDITION

With an Appendix on Modern Technique by

MAX VOGRICH

G. SCHIRMER, Inc.

DISTRIBUTED BY

HAL•LEONARD®
CORPORATION

7777 W. BLUEMOUND RD. P.O.BOX 13819 MILWAUKEE, WI 53213

2

I.
Exercises for rendering the fingers independent of each other.

In exercises NOS 1–29 the whole notes must not be struck, but the corresponding keys are to be held down firmly in such a way that their tones never sound with that of the active finger. — Besides this, the exercises should, at first, be played very slowly, repeating each separate number from 8 to 10 times, and accelerating the tempo only to an extent fully warranted by the increasing strength and supple flexibility of the fingers.

I.
Uebungen, um die Finger von einander unabhängig zu machen.

Bei den Uebungen № 1–29 dürfen die ganzen Noten nicht angeschlagen, sondern nur so fest niedergehalten werden, dass die Tasten, welche sie einnehmen, niemals mit erklingen. — Uebrigens beobachte man Anfangs ein sehr langsames Zeitmass, wiederhole jede einzelne Nummer acht bis zehn mal und vermehre die Schnelligkeit nur in dem Grade, als die Kraft und geschmeidige Beweglichkeit der Finger bemerkbar wird.

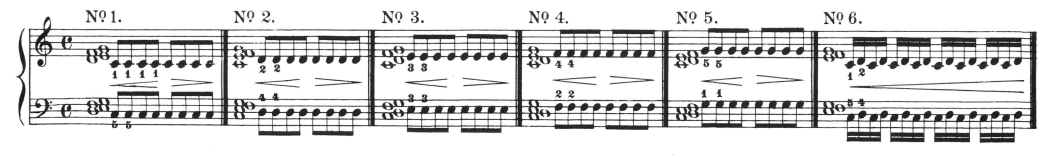

11327

Printed in the U.S.A.

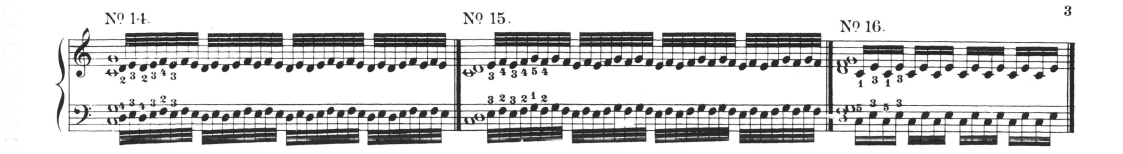

II.
Exercises on the Trill.

Practice of the Trill is necessary, not only because this grace occurs in almost every piece of music, but because it is the readiest means for acquiring both evenness and firmness of touch. It will, therefore, be of the greatest benefit to the pupil to practise the following exercises assiduously, and, at first, very slowly, with each hand alone, and so distinctly that each of the two tones makes a separate impression on the ear.

A good execution of the Trill depends solely on the well-regulated movement of the fingers, whose activity centres chiefly in the knuckle-joint; any motion whatever of the hand would act as a disturbing element.

II.
Triller- Uebungen.

Das Ueben der Triller ist nicht allein darum nothwendig, weil diese Verzierung fast in jedem Musikstück vorkommt, sondern auch, weil man dadurch vorzüglich den Fingern eine gewisse Gleichheit und Festigkeit im Anschlag verschafft. Es wird daher den Schülern grossen Nutzen gewähren, wenn sie die nachfolgenden Sätzchen fleissig spielen und zwar Anfangs sehr langsam, mit jeder Hand allein und so deutlich, dass jeder von den beiden Tönen dem Ohre stets abgesondert vorschwebt.

Die gute Ausführung der Triller beruht ausschliesslich auf einer wohl abgemessenen Bewegung der Finger, deren obere Gelenke am meisten dabei thätig sein müssen; dagegen würde jede Bewegung der Hand hier nur störend einwirken.

*) It is advantageous to play Nos 30–35 through several times without a break at a uniform rate of speed.

*) Es ist vortheilhaft, die Nummern 30—35 öfters ohne Unterbrechung in einem gleichmässigen Tempo fortzuspielen.

III.

Five-finger Exercises
within the compass of 5 notes.

Exercises on 5 successive notes, in which the hand retains one and the same position, are commonly termed Exercises with Quiet Hand.

The best teachers of recent times are unanimous in considering them the most important means for many-sided finger-practice, and for properly and thoroughly developing the finger-action.

However, in order to derive real benefit from them, they must be studied in the most conscientious and persevering manner. To begin with, all the notes must be played evenly, and without any motion whatever in the hand and arm, in very slow tempo; as the strength and freedom of the fingers increase, the exercises may be played faster and faster, and in different degrees of loudness and softness (as shown in No. 36.)

The natural inclination of the hand toward the little-finger side should be neutralized by inclining it in the opposite direction, i.e., somewhat toward the thumb.

It is equally important to leave the fingers on the keys no longer than the due time; at the precise instant that one strikes its key, the other should be lifted.

III.

Uebungen der fünf Finger
in dem Raume von 5 Tönen.

Die Uebungen, welche Notenreihen von 5 Tönen darbieten und wobei die Hand stets ein und dieselbe Lage beibehält, nennt man gewöhnlich Uebungen mit stillstehender oder ruhiger Hand.

Nach dem Urtheil aller besseren, Lehrer der neuesten Zeit sind sie unbedingt das wichtigste Mittel, die Finger vielseitig zu beschäftigen und somit einen schönen Mechanismus zu erlangen.

Um jedoch den wahren Nutzen daraus zu ziehen, muss man sich ein sehr sorgfältiges und anhaltendes Studium derselben zur Pflicht machen. Zuvörderst müssen alle Noten mit Gleichheit und ohne alle Bewegung der Hand oder des Armes, ganz langsam, in der Folge aber—sowie die Finger an Kraft und Freiheit gewinnen—immer schneller und in verschiedenen Graden der Stärke und Schwäche(nach Angabe des Beispiels No. 36) ausgeführt werden.

Dabei ist das, der Hand so natürliche, Hinneigen nach dem fünften Finger ganz besonders zu vermeiden und durch das Gegentheil zu beseitigen, indem man die Hand mehr nach dem Daumen hinwendet.

Eben so wichtig ist es, die Finger nicht länger als nöthig auf den Tasten liegen zu lassen; denn in dem Augenblick als ein Finger auf seine Taste niederfällt, muss sich der andre sogleich frei erheben.

No. 36.

6

⌒) The first note of each triplet must be slightly accented. | *) Die erste Note jeder Triole muss ein wenig stärker gespielt werden.

No 52. *)

No 53.

No 54.

No 55.

No 56.

No 57.

No 58.

No 59.

*) The first note of each Sextuplet should be slightly accented.

*) Die erste Note einer jeden Sextole wird ein wenig markirt.

№ 60.

№ 61.

№ 62.

№ 63.

№ 64.

№ 65.

№ 66.

№ 67.

№ 68.

№ 69.

№ 70.

№ 71.

№ 72

№ 73.

№ 74.

№ 75.

№ 76.

№ 77.

№ 78.

№ 79.

№ 80.

№ 81.

№ 82.

№ 83.

Nº 84. Nº 85.

Nº 86. Nº 87.

Nº 88. Nº 89.

Nº 90. Nº 91.

Nº 92.

Nº 93.

Nº 94.

Nº 95.

Nº 96.

Nº 97.

Nº 98.

Nº 99.

№ 100. № 101.

№ 102.

№ 103. № 104.

№ 105.

IV.

Thirds and other paired notes, with quiet hand.

Practice in striking two notes at once, especially thirds, is peculiarly adapted for acquiring firmness in the hand, energy of finger-stroke, and consequent precision in touch.

The inclination so often manifested at first, to play such paired notes one after the other instead of exactly together, or to strike them with unequal force, must be conquered by persevering effort, otherwise the object in view will be frustrated.

IV.

Terzen und andere Doppelgriffe mit ruhender Hand.

Die Doppelgriffe, besonders die Terzen, sind ganz dazu geeignet, der Hand Festigkeit, den Fingern Energie und dadurch dem Spieler Präcision im Anschlage zu verschaffen.

Der, Anfangs sehr gewöhnlichen, Neigung die Doppelgriffe zu brechen, oder dieselben mit ungleicher Stärke anzuschlagen, muss man durchaus zu widerstreben suchen, weil sonst der bestimmte Zweck verfehlt wird.

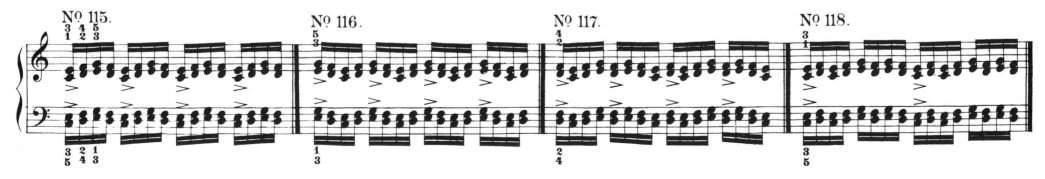

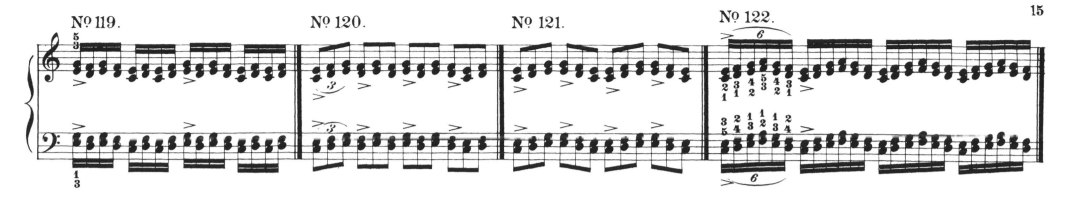

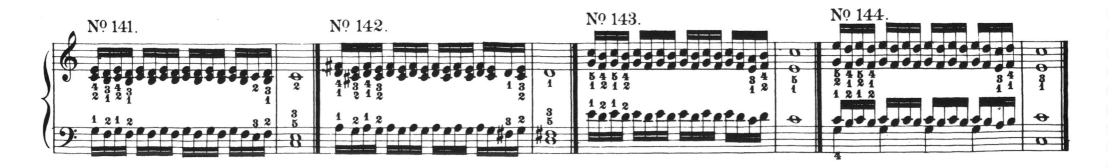

Advancing the hands in figures repeated on successive degrees.

The following exercises are intended to accustom the hand to retain its correct position (i. e., perfectly quiet, and bent slightly outwards) on the keyboard when playing either up or down. In such passages, a fingering should be chosen which permits of repetition; this renders the execution more even.

Fortrücken der Hände bei Figuren, welche stufenweise sich wiederholen.

Durch die folgenden Uebungssätze soll die Hand gewöhnt werden, ihre richtige (d. i. völlig ruhige und auswärts gebogene) Haltung auf der Tastatur in auf- und abwärts gehender Bewegung zu behaupten. Bei dergleichen Stellen muss man immer einen Fingersatz zu wählen suchen, welcher sich wiederholen lässt; der Vortrag gewinnt dadurch an Gleichheit.

№ 145. *) In Thirds. — In Terzen.

№ 146. In Sixths. — In Sexten.

№ 147. In Octaves. — In Oktaven.

№ 148. In Tenths. — In Decimen.

№ 149.

№ 150.

№ 151.

*) Extend the range of these Exercises through several octaves.

*) Man spiele diese Uebungen im Umfange von mehreren Octaven.

No 152.

No 153.

No 154.

№ 155.

№ 156.

№ 157.   № 158.

№ 159.   № 160.

N⁰ 161.

N⁰ 162.

N⁰ 163.

the same descending.
(eben so zurück.)

the same descending.
(eben so zurück.)

N⁰ 164.

N⁰ 165.

N⁰ 166.

the same descending.
(eben so zurück.)

the same descending.
(eben so zurück.)

Nº 167. Nº 168.

the same descending. (eben so zurück.)

the same descending.
(eben so zurück.)

Nº 169. Nº 170.

the same descending.
(eben so zurück.)

the same descending.
(eben so zurück.)

Nº 171. Nº 172. In paired notes. — In Doppelgriffen.

cresc. decresc.

Nº 173. Nº 174. the same descending.
(eben so zurück.)

Nº 175.

the same descending.
(eben so zurück.)

Nº 176.

Nº 177.

Nº 178.

Nº 179.

Nº 180.

Compare Appendix Nº 1.
(Siehe Anhang Nº 1.)

VI.

Preparatory Exercises for the Scales.

As soon as the pupil has acquired uniformity and evenness in finger-action through the practice of the Exercises in Book I of this Collection, he may take up the Preparatory Exercises for the Scales.

These consist, as shown in the next 14 examples, in learning to pass the thumb under the 2nd, 3rd and 4th fingers, and said fingers over the thumb, with dexterity. To attain this end, perfect quietness of the hand and arm during practice must be insisted on, and the thumb (which is somewhat bent) must be taught to pass under the fingers with such complete freedom and independence, that neither any separation of the two tones, nor any unevenness in touch, is perceptible. Arrived at this point, the pupil will not find the Scales difficult, and their practice will be of real benefit to him.

VI.

Vorübungen zu den Tonleitern.

Wenn sich der Schüler durch die im ersten Hefte dieser Collection enthaltenen Uebungen mit ruhender Hand eine gleichmässige Ausbildung der Finger erworben hat, so mögen die Vorübungen zu den Tonleitern beginnen.

Diese bestehen zufolge der Beispiele 1 bis 14 darin, dass man das Untersetzen des Daumens unter den zweiten, dritten und vierten Finger, sowie das Uebersetzen derselben über den Daumen mit Geläufigkeit vollziehen lerne. Um dahin zu gelangen, muss man beim Ueben die ruhige Haltung der Hand und des Armes nie vernachlässigen und den etwas gebogenen Daumen so selbstständig unter den Fingern hin und her zu bewegen sich bemühen, dass zuletzt keine Trennung der beiden Töne, noch Ungleichheit im Anschlage zu hören ist. Alsdann werden die Tonleitern nicht mehr schwierig erscheinen und auch wirklichen Nutzen gewähren.

*) The whole notes are to be held down, but not struck. — Die ganzen Noten werden gehalten, aber nicht angeschlagen.

No 191.

No 192.

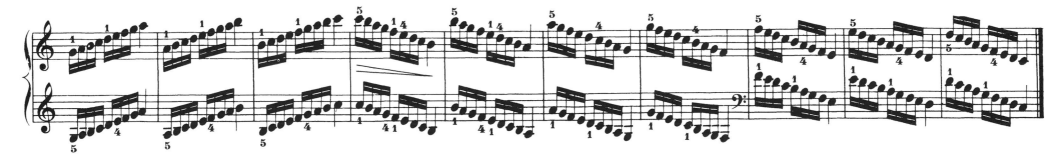

No 193.

No 194.

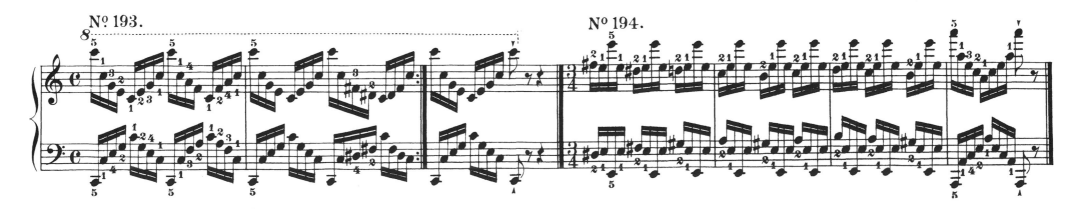

VII.

Major and Minor Scales.

Play each scale, at first, with one hand alone, then with perfect evenness with both hands together, so that each tone sounds as loud as the rest. Avoid all haste, and proceed very cautiously and gradually to a more rapid rate of execution. When the fingering is thoroughly learned, run the Scales through the compass of the keyboard, repeating each several times without a break, and executing it in piano, forte, crescendo and decrescendo.

Besides the practical execution of the Scales, the pupil should also be taught their theory; this is indispensable for a complete understanding of their construction.

VII.

Die Dur- und Moll-Tonleitern.

Man spiele Anfangs jede Tonleiter mit einer Hand allein, alsdann ganz gleichmässig mit beiden Händen zusammen und lasse stets einen Ton wie den andern deutlich klingen. Dabei vermeide man alles Eilen und gehe nur behutsam und gradweise zur schnellern Ausführung über. Nach erlangter Sicherheit im Fingersatze durchlaufe man die ganze Klaviatur und wiederhole jede Tonleiter oft und ohne Unterbrechung, indem man bald piano, bald forte, bald crescendo und decrescendo spielt.

Neben der praktischen Ausübung erkläre der Lehrer seinen Schülern zugleich auch den theoretischen Theil der Tonleiter: dies ist zum vollkommnen Verständniss der Sache unentbehrlich.

No 195. C major. _ C dur.*) No 196. A minor. _ A moll.

No 197. G major. _ G dur. No 198. E minor. _ E moll.

*)For beginners with scale-practice it is often beneficial, for a time, at least, to make a brief pause on the key-note, thus:

*)Für Anfänger dürfte es zweckmässig sein, eine Zeit lang die Tonleitern so zu spielen, dass sie jedesmal beim Grundton derselben etwas anhalten, z.B.

№ 199. D major._D dur.

№ 200. B minor. _ H moll.

№ 201. A major._A dur.

№ 202. F♯ minor. _ Fis moll.

№ 203. E major._E dur.

№ 204. C♯ minor._Cis moll.

№ 205. B major._H dur.

№ 206. G♯ minor._Gis moll.

Nº 207. F♯ major._Fis dur.

Nº 208. D♯ minor._Dis moll.

Nº 209. D♭ major._Des dur.

Nº 210. B♭ minor._B moll.

Nº 211. A♭ major._As dur.

Nº 212. F minor._F moll.

Nº 213. E♭ major._Es dur.

Nº 214. C minor._C moll.

Nº 215. B♭ major._B dur.

Nº 216. G minor._G moll.

Nº 217. F major._F dur.

Nº 218. D minor._D moll.

VIII.

The Scales at various Intervals, and in contrary motion.

When the pupil has become sufficiently familiar with the preceding 24 Scales, it will be found highly conducive to his skill in scale-playing to let him practice them in thirds, sixths, and in contrary motion.

To save room, the scales in tenths are omitted, their fingering being identical with that of the scales in thirds.

VIII.

Die Tonleitern in verschiedenen Intervallen und Bewegungen.

Hat man sich mit den vorhergehenden 24 Tonleitern hinlänglich vertraut gemacht, so ist es, zur Vermehrung der Gewandheit, sehr nützlich, dieselben in der Terz. Decime, Sexte und in der Gegenbewegung zu üben._

Um Raum zu ersparen sind die Tonleitern in der Decime, da sie ohnehin ganz gleichen Fingersatz mit denen in der Terz haben, weggelassen worden.

Nº 219. C major in Thirds._C dur in Terzen.

Nº 220. C minor in Thirds._C moll in Terzen.

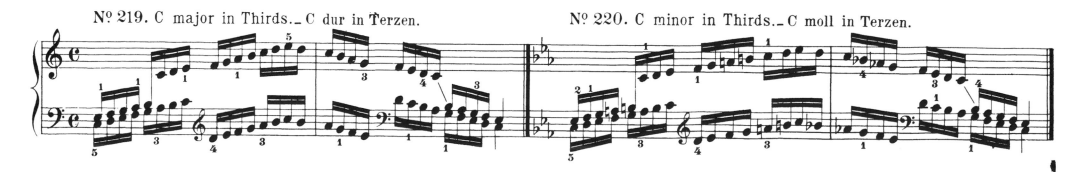

Nº 221. In Sixths._ In Sexten.

Nº 222. In Sixths._In Sexten.

Nº 223. G major in Thirds._G dur in Terzen.

Nº 224. G minor in Thirds._G moll in Terzen.

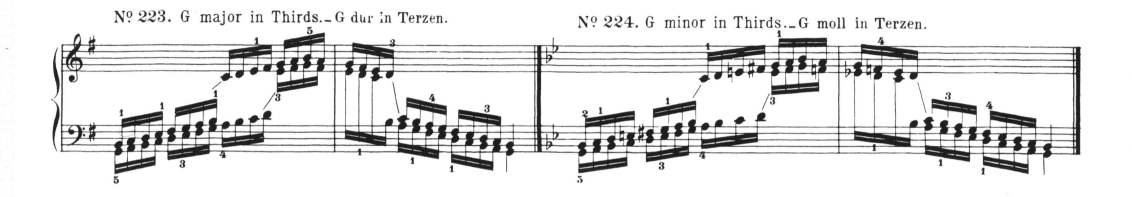

Nº 225. In Sixths._In Sexten.

Nº 226. In Sixths._In Sexten.

№ 227. D major in Thirds._ D dur in Terzen.   № 228. D minor in Thirds._ D moll in Terzen.

№ 229. In Sixths._ In Sexten.   № 230. In Sixths._ In Sexten.

№ 231. A major in Thirds._ A dur in Terzen.   № 232. A minor in Thirds._ A moll in Terzen.

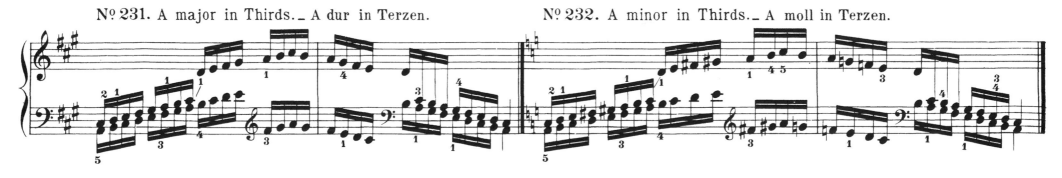

№ 233. In Sixths._ In Sexten.   № 234. In Sixths._ In Sexten.

№ 235. E major in Thirds.—E dur in Terzen. № 236. E minor in Thirds.—E moll in Terzen.

№ 237. In Sixths.— In Sexten. № 238. In Sixths.— In Sexten.

№ 239. B major in Thirds.—H dur in Terzen. № 240. B minor in Thirds.—H moll in Terzen.

№ 241. In Sixths.— In Sexten. № 242. In Sixths.— In Sexten.

Nº 243. F# major in Thirds._Fis dur in Terzen.   Nº 244. F# minor in Thirds._Fis moll in Terzen.

Nº 245. In Sixths._In Sexten.   Nº 246. In Sixths._In Sexten.

Nº 247. Db major in Thirds._Des dur in Terzen.   Nº 248. C# minor in Thirds._Cis moll in Terzen.

Nº 249. In Sixths._In Sexten.   Nº 250. In Sixths._In Sexten.

№ 251. A♭ major in Thirds._As dur in Terzen.   № 252. G♯ minor in Thirds._Gis moll in Terzen.

№ 253. In Sixths._In Sexten.   № 254. In Sixths._In Sexten.

№ 255. E♭ major in Thirds._Es dur in Terzen.   №256. D♯ minor in Thirds._Dis moll in Terzen.

№ 257. In Sixths._In Sexten.   № 258. In Sixths._In Sexten.

Nº 259. Bb major in Thirds.—B dur in Terzen.

Nº 260. Bb minor in Thirds.—B moll in Terzen.

Nº 261. In Sixths.—In Sexten.

Nº 262. In Sixths.—In Sexten.

Nº 263. F major in Thirds.—F dur in Terzen.

Nº 264. F minor in Thirds.—F moll in Terzen.

Nº 265. In Sixths.—In Sexten.

Nº 266. In Sixths.—In Sexten.

Nº 267. Ascending in Tenths and descending in Sixths.—Im Aufsteigen in Decimen und im Absteigen in Sexten.

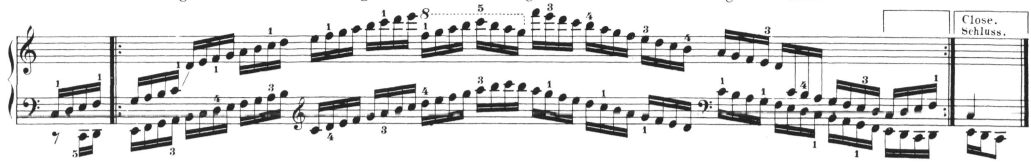

Nº 268. Ascending in Sixths and descending in Tenths.—Im Aufsteigen in Sexten und im Absteigen in Decimen.

Nº 269. In contrary motion.—In der Gegenbewegung.

Nº 270.

Beginning on the unison.—Mit dem Einklange anfangend.

Nº 271.　　　　　　　　　　　**Nº 272.**

Beginning with the Third.—Mit der Terz anfangend.

Note. Exercises **267** to **274** inclusive should be transposed into all the other major and minor keys; the fingering is to correspond to that given for the preceding scales.

Anm. Die Beispiele Nº **267** bis **274** trage man auf alle übrigen Dur- und Molltonleitern über; wobei stets der, in den vorhergegangenen Tonleitern angegebene Fingersatz gewählt werden kann.

Nº 273.

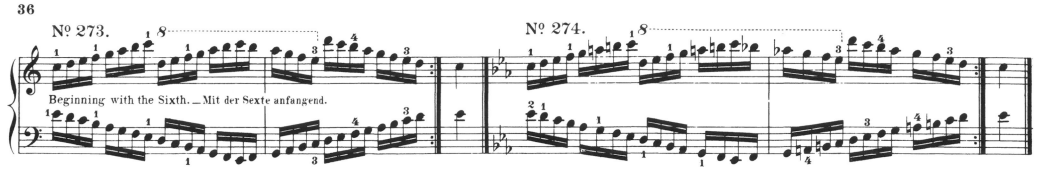

Beginning with the Sixth._Mit der Sexte anfangend.

Nº 274.

IX.

Chromatic Scale._Chromatische Tonleiter.

Nº 275. In Octaves._In Octaven.

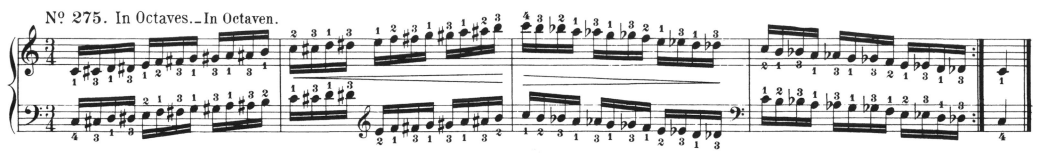

Nº 276. In Thirds._In Terzen.

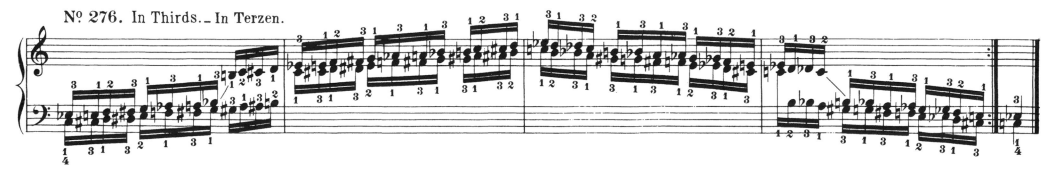

Nº 277. In Sixths._In Sexten.

№ 278. In contrary motion._In der Gegenbewegung.

Note. Besides the fingering given here, which, by reason of its similarity for both hands, may be regarded as the standard, two other fingerings are frequently met with, prescribed by great masters of piano-playing either in instruction-books or in compositions (compare the next example). These must also be learned by every good player; for cases are not rare in which they can be profitably applied.

Anm. Ausser der hier vorgeschriebenen Fingersetzung, welche wegen ihrer Gleichförmigkeit für beide Hände, als Regel gelten kann, findet man von grossen Meistern des Piano-Spiels theils in Lehrbüchern, theils in Musikstücken selbst, noch häufig zwei andere Arten des Fingersatzes angegeben. (Siehe die folgenden Beispiele). Diese muss sich jeder gute Spieler ebenfalls aneignen; denn die Fälle, wo er einen vortheilhaften Gebrauch davon machen kann, sind nicht selten.

№ 279.

№ 280.

X.

a) In Triads._ In Dreiklängen.   Exercises in Broken Chords. _ Beispiele von gebrochenen Akkorden.

№ 281. C major._ C dur.

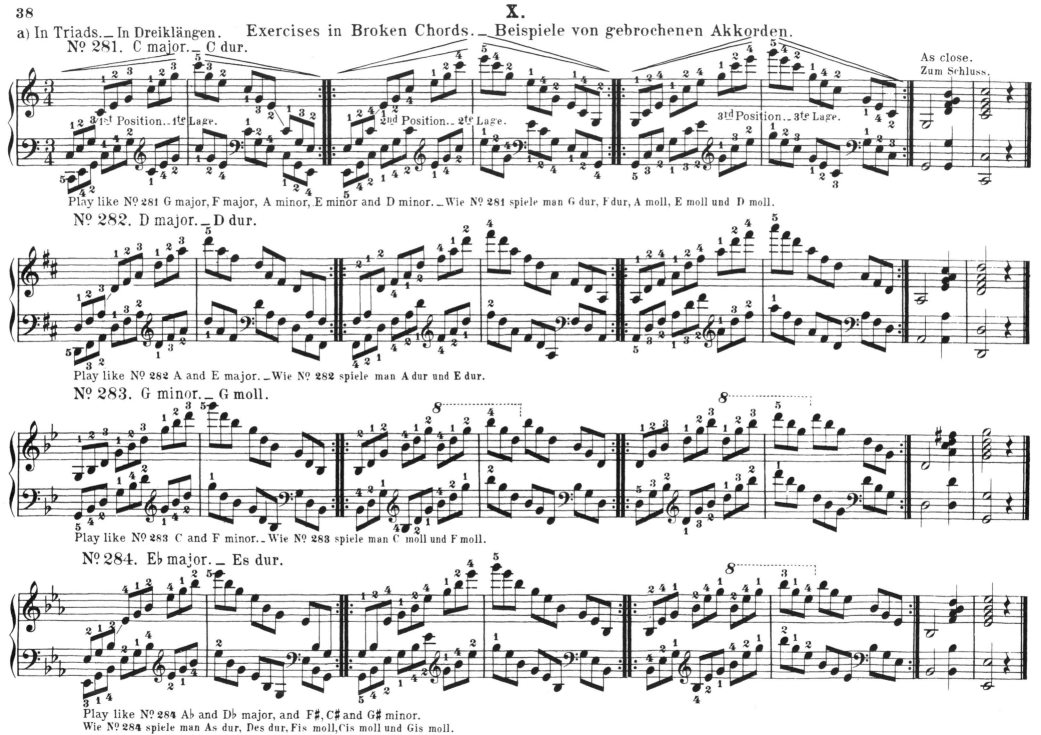

Play like № 281 G major, F major, A minor, E minor and D minor. _ Wie № 281 spiele man G dur, F dur, A moll, E moll und D moll.

№ 282. D major._ D dur.

Play like № 282 A and E major. _ Wie № 282 spiele man A dur und E dur.

№ 283. G minor._ G moll.

Play like № 283 C and F minor. _ Wie № 283 spiele man C moll und F moll.

№ 284. E♭ major._ Es dur.

Play like № 284 A♭ and D♭ major, and F♯, C♯ and G♯ minor.
Wie № 284 spiele man As dur, Des dur, Fis moll, Cis moll und Gis moll.

Nº 285. B♭ major._ B dur.

Nº 286. B♭ minor._ B moll.

Nº 287. G♭ major._ Ges dur.

Nº 288. E♭ minor._ Es moll.

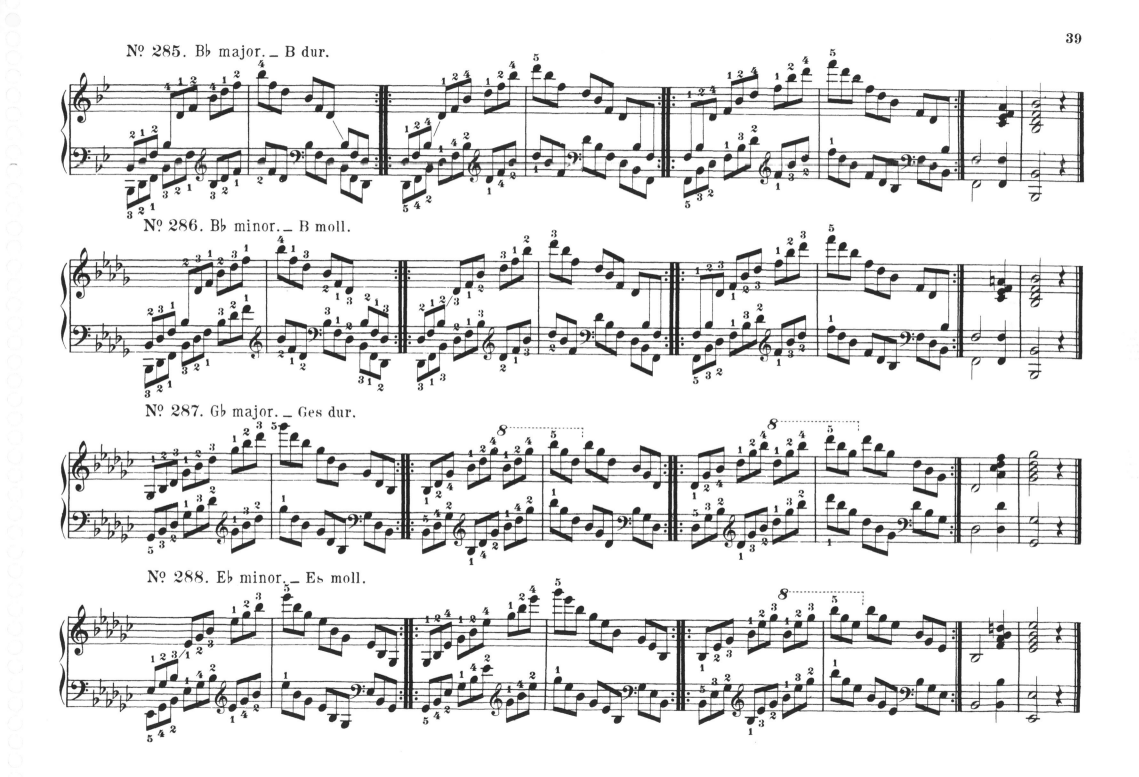

40

Nº 289. B major. _ H dur.

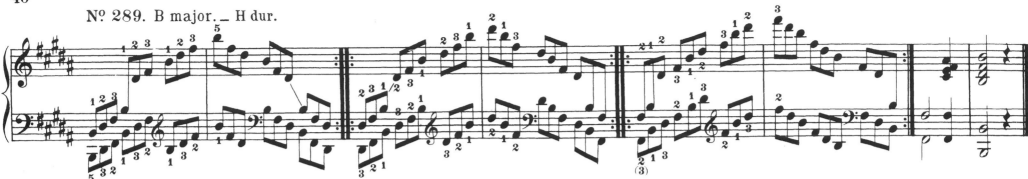

Nº 290. B minor. _ H moll.

Nº 291.

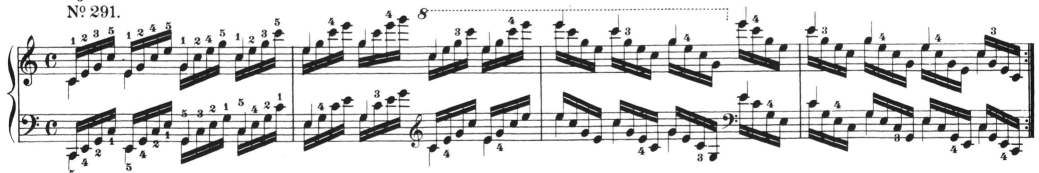

Nº 292.　　　　　　　　　　　　　Nº 293.

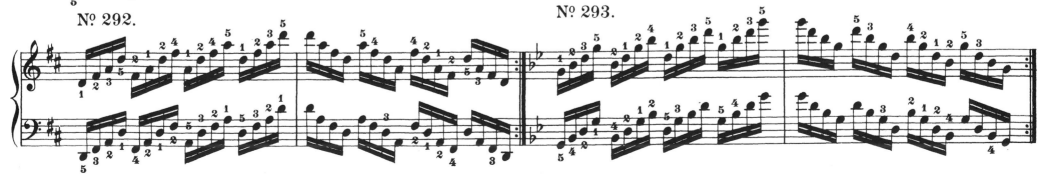

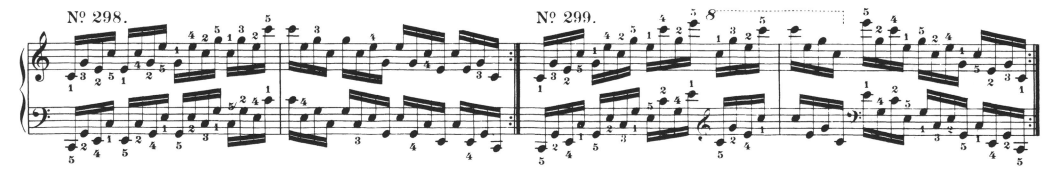

№ 302.

№ 303.

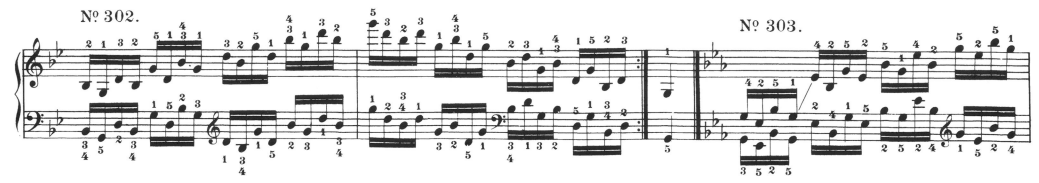

b) In Chords of the Seventh. — In Septimenakkorden.

*) № 304.

1st Position. — 1te Lage.   2nd Position. — 2te Lage.

3rd Position. — 3te Lage.   4th Position. — 4te Lage.

№ 305.

*) Extend Exercises 304 to 307 through a range of several octaves.

*) Man spiele diese Uebungen von № 304 bis 307 im Umfange von mehreren Octaven.

No. 306.

No. 307.

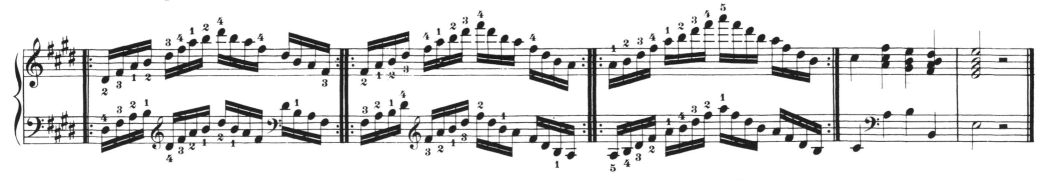

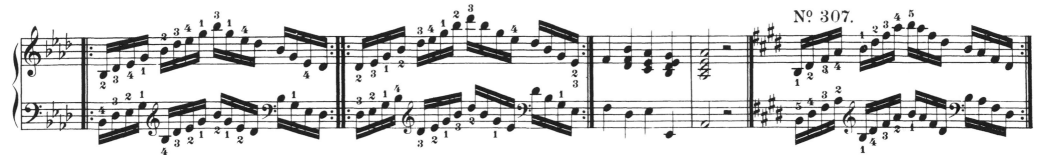

No. 308.

No. 309.

Fingering of the modern school._ Fingersatz der neuern Schule.

No. 310.

No. 311.

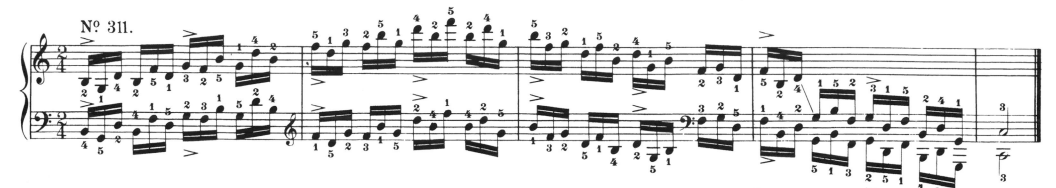

No. 312.

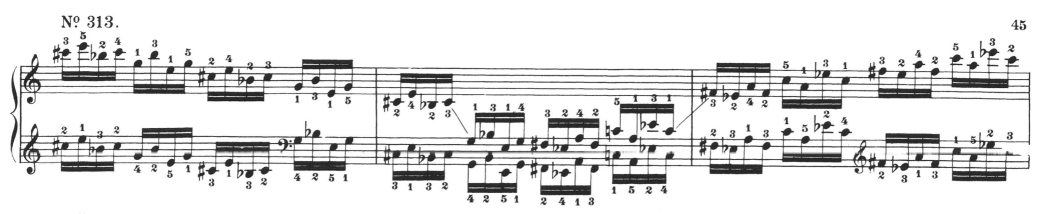

No 314.*)

The same descending.
Eben so zurück.

*) This is an excellent exercise for the stretched Position of the fingers; the fingers should hold their respective keys as long as possible.

*) Dieses Beispiel ist für die ausgestreckte Lage der Hand eine sehr gute Uebung, wobei man aber die Finger so lange als möglich auf den Tasten liegen lassen muss.

XI.
Scales in Thirds.

XI.
Terzen. _ Tonleitern.

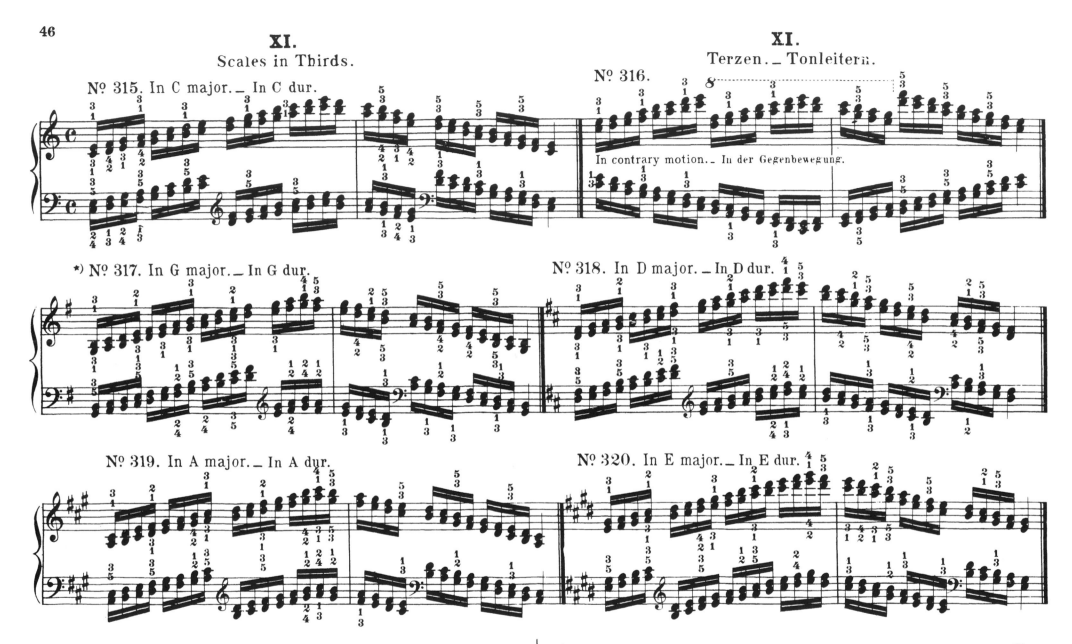

Nº 315. In C major. _ In C dur.

Nº 316.

In contrary motion. _ In der Gegenbewegung.

*) Nº 317. In G major. _ In G dur.

Nº 318. In D major. _ In D dur.

Nº 319. In A major. _ In A dur.

Nº 320. In E major. _ In E dur.

*) The fingering given in Exercises 317 to 331 <u>over</u> the thirds is advantageous on account of its peculiar regularity, inasmuch as it allows the hands, when playing together, to change their position simultaneously. This greatly facilitates the practice of such passages, and a certain evenness in their execution is attained. _ However, the fingering <u>under</u> the thirds, which frequently differs from that above, is permissible, and not seldom preferable to the latter, especially for passages in thirds for one hand alone.

*) Der Fingersatz, welcher in den Beispielen Nº 317 bis 331 über den Terzen steht, gewährt den Vortheil einer besonderen Regelmässigkeit, insofern er den Händen gestattet, beim Zusammenspiel die Lage gleichzeitig zu ändern. Hierdurch wird das Einüben solcher Stellen sehr erleichtert und eine gewisse Gleichheit in der Ausführung erreicht. _ Jedoch ist auch der <u>unter</u> den Terzen stehende, häufig von dem oberen abweichende Fingersatz zulässig und in vielen Fällen wohl brauchbarer, vorzüglich bei Terzenpassagen für eine Hand allein.

Nº 321. In F major. _ In F dur.

Nº 322. In B♭ major. _ In B dur.

Nº 323. In E♭ major. _ In Es dur.

Nº 324. In A♭ major. _ In As dur.

Nº 325. In A minor. _ In A moll.

Nº 326. In E minor. _ In E moll.

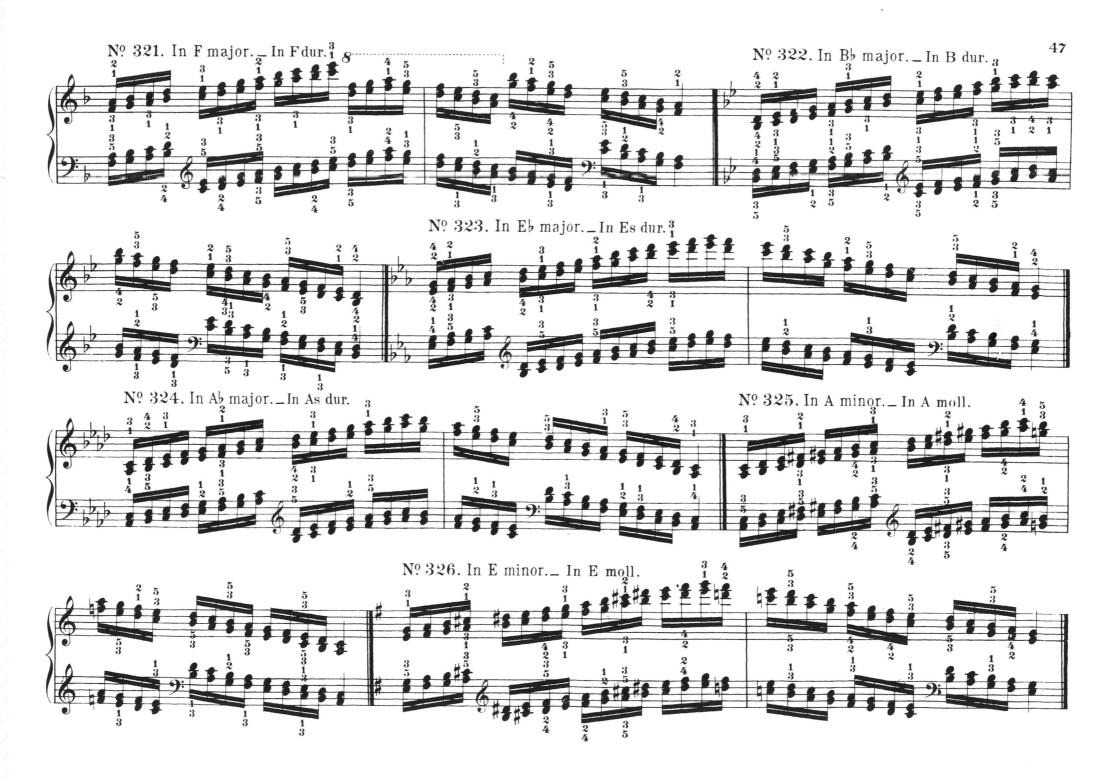

48

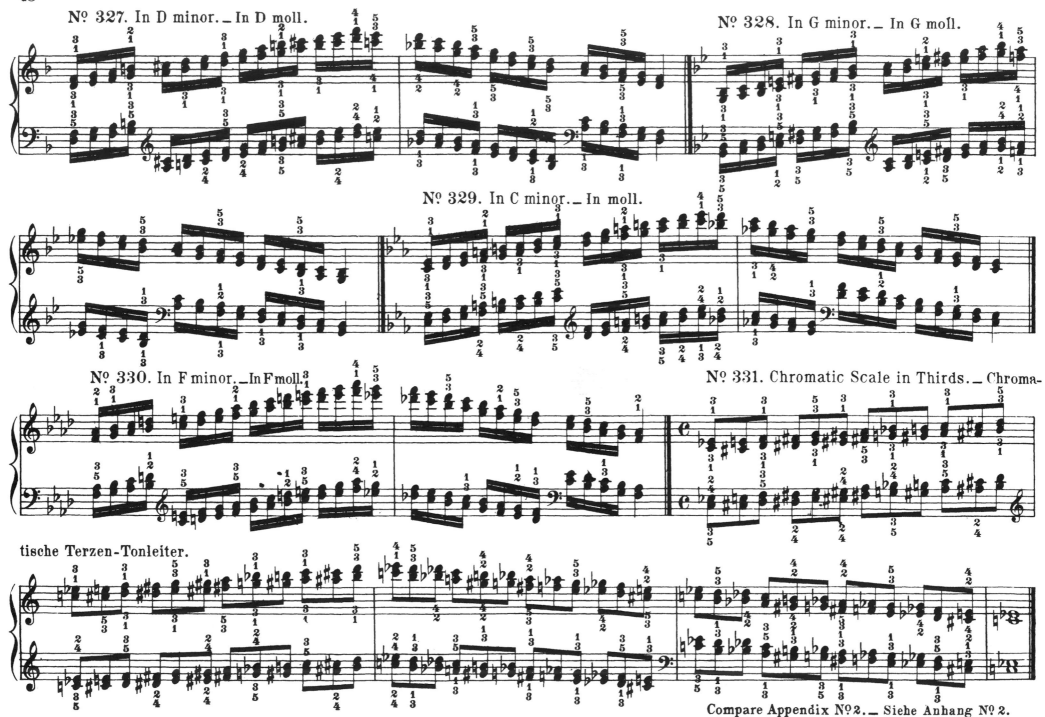

Nº 327. In D minor.__In D moll.

Nº 328. In G minor.__In G moll.

Nº 329. In C minor.__In moll.

Nº 330. In F minor.__In F moll.

Nº 331. Chromatic Scale in Thirds.__Chroma-

tische Terzen-Tonleiter.

Compare Appendix Nº 2.__ Siehe Anhang Nº 2.

XII.
Exercises for the Wrist.

For staccato thirds, sixths, and octaves, lightness and endurance are desirable qualities. They are most readily acquired, not by practicing with a stiff arm, but with the stroke from the wrist, i.e., the raising and depressing of the hand alone.

XII.
Uebungen mit dem Handgelenk.

Bei abgestossenen Terzen, Sexten und Octaven sind Leichtigkeit und Ausdauer zwei wünschenswerthe Eigenschaften. Man erlangt dieselben am sichersten dadurch, dass man nicht mit steifem Arme übt, sondern den Anschlag mehr vermittelst des Handgelenks (d.i. durch Heben und Senken der Hand) bewerkstelligt.

Nº 341.   Nº 342.   Nº 343.   Nº 344.

Nº 345.   Nº 346.   Nº 347.

Nº 348.   Nº 349.

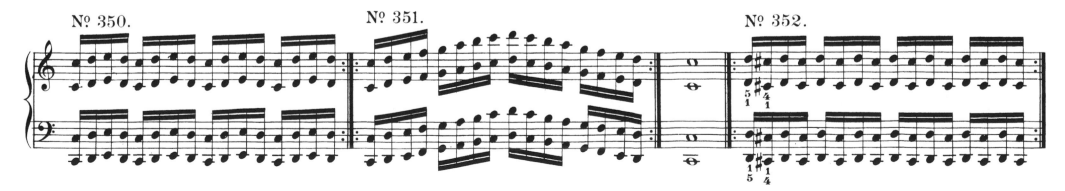

Nº 350.   Nº 351.   Nº 352.

№ 353.
№ 354.
№ 355.

№ 356.
№ 357.

№ 358.
№ 359.

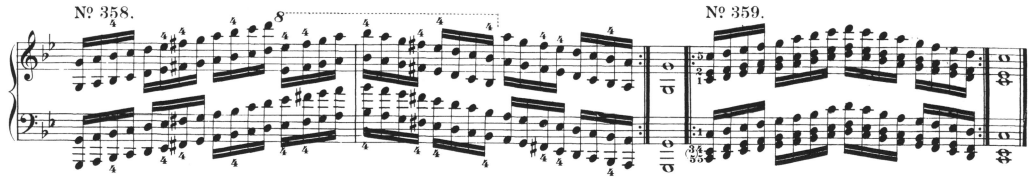

№ 360.
№ 361.

Appendix № I.
Additions by Max Vogrich.

Anhang № I.
Ergänzungen von Max Vogrich.

№ 1. Elasticity. – Spannkraft.

№ 2.

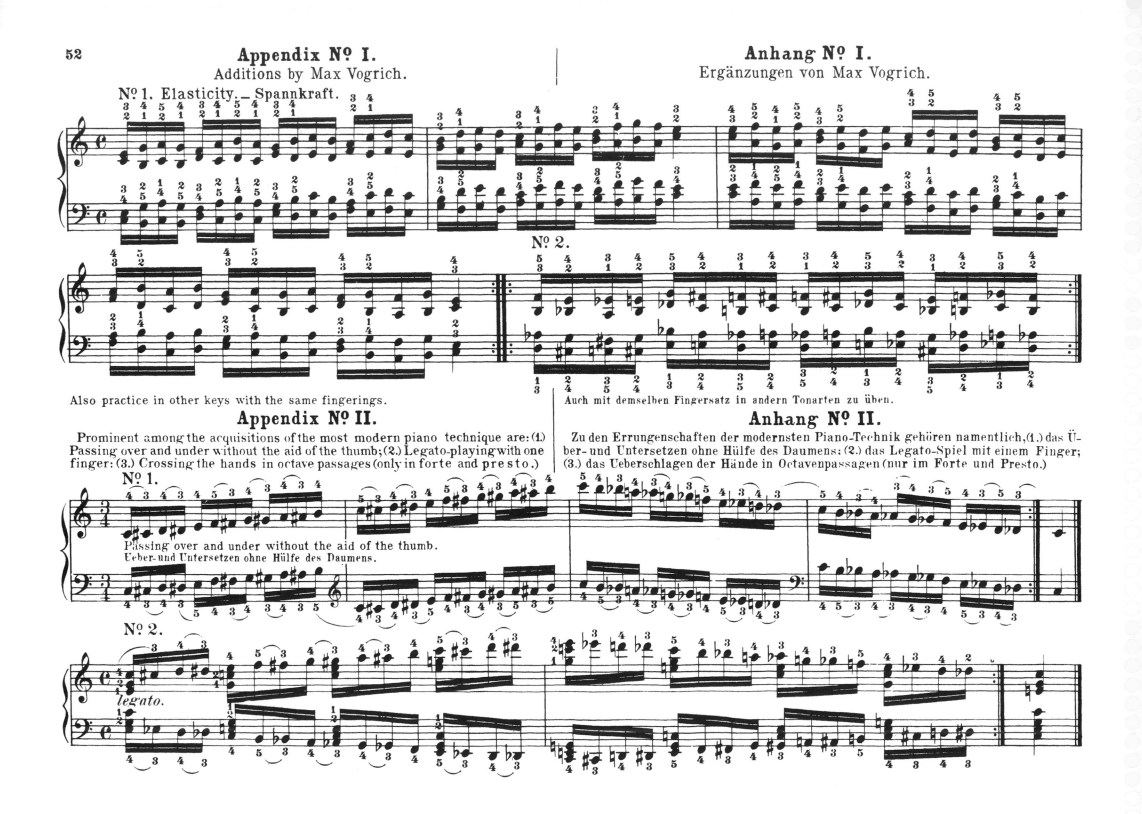

Also practice in other keys with the same fingerings.

Auch mit demselben Fingersatz in andern Tonarten zu üben.

Appendix № II.

Prominent among the acquisitions of the most modern piano technique are: (1.) Passing over and under without the aid of the thumb; (2.) Legato-playing with one finger: (3.) Crossing the hands in octave passages (only in forte and presto.)

Anhang № II.

Zu den Errungenschaften der modernsten Piano-Technik gehören namentlich, (1.) das Über- und Untersetzen ohne Hülfe des Daumens; (2.) das Legato-Spiel mit einem Finger; (3.) das Ueberschlagen der Hände in Octavenpassagen (nur im Forte und Presto.)

№ 1.

Passing over and under without the aid of the thumb.
Ueber- und Untersetzen ohne Hülfe des Daumens.

№ 2.

legato.

Legato-playing with one finger. _ Legato-Spiel mit einem Finger.

53

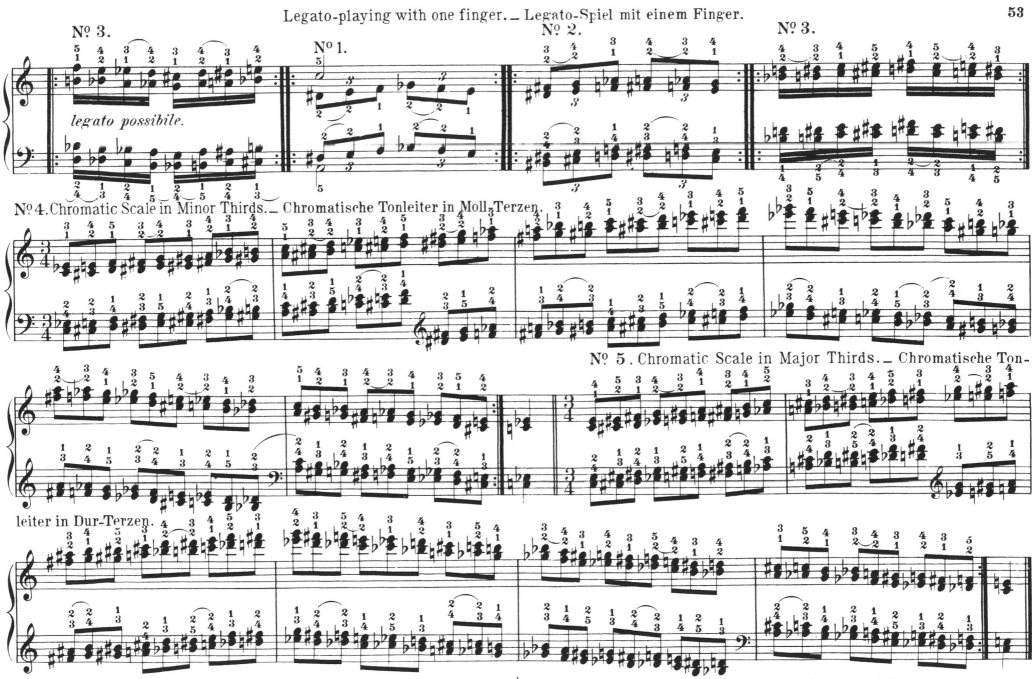

No. 3. No. 1. No. 2. No. 3.

No. 4. Chromatic Scale in Minor Thirds. _ Chromatische Tonleiter in Moll-Terzen.

No. 5. Chromatic Scale in Major Thirds. _ Chromatische Ton-

leiter in Dur-Terzen.

This fingering of the chromatic scale in major and minor thirds is the only one permitting of an absolutely flawless legato. The old fingering, even when the utmost pains are taken, succeeds at best in deceiving the ear.

Diese Fingersetzung der chromatischen Tonleiter in Dur und Moll-Terzen ist die einzige welche ein absolut vollkommenes Legato zulässt. Mit Anwendung des alten Systems kann man es bei grösster Mühe doch nur zu einer Ohrentäuschung bringen.

Crossing the Hands in Chord-passages and Octave-passages.

Ueberschlagen der Hande in Accord= und Octavenpassagen.

This style of technique is effective only in very rapid tempo, combined with forte. The earlier masters made no use of it; all the more, examples are found in the works of modern virtuosi, more especially Liszt, Henselt, and Rubinstein.

Derlei Technik ist nur im sehr raschen Tempo und Forte von Wirkung. Die älteren Meister enthielten sich derselben gänzlich; desto mehr findet man davon in den Werken der modernen Virtuosen, namentlich Liszt, Henselt und Rubinstein.

0-73999-93366-6

HL50253210

G. SCHIRMER, *Inc.*

DISTRIBUTED BY

U.S. $12.99

ISBN 978-1-4234-9224-5

51299